# ARBOR VITAE

&

To Arthur Sherman
with pleasure at meeting
and with Thanks for
the St. John's reading —

Jane Augustine

19.X.05

# ARBOR VITAE

☙

JANE AUGUSTINE

☙

MARSH HAWK PRESS ❧ NEW YORK ❧ 2002

First Edition
02 03 7 6 5 4 3 2 1

Marsh Hawk Press books are published by Poetry Mailing List, Inc.,
a not-for-profit corporation under United States
Internal Revenue Code.

Cover Art: Jane Augustine
Book Design: Sandy McIntosh
Printed in the United States by McNaughton & Gunn

Acknowledgements (some titles differ slightly): "East Hampton: Nearly Midnight" and
"The Next Midnight, Even Quieter" appeared in Confrontation 30 (1999). Part of "Re-
entry" appeared in Poetry New York #8, Spring 1996; "Sunday Morning" and
"Metaphysics II" in Archae 4, 1992; "[Untitled: My Brother]" in Poetry New
York,Winter 1991/ Spring 1992; and "Broken Meditation" in Poetry Brook, Spring
1991, Stony Brook (L.I., NY). The following poems appeared in French Windows
(1998) in the Poetry New York Pamphlet Series, Tod Thilleman, editor: "From a Paris
Sketchbook", "Notre Dame de Blanc-Manteaux", "In a Dream My Mother", "After the
Museums, From a Window, Late Afternoon", "Interior: Midnight", "Stone Water-
trough at a Crossroads in Provence", "In Provence, Near Venasque: Le Beaucet",
"Ghazal at a Rainy Window, 2 p.m.", "In the Dark Garden—10:30 p.m.", "Une
Américaine à Paris", "The Louvre: Egyptian Antiquities"

Library of Congress Cataloging-in-Publication Data

Augustine, Jane.
Arbor vitae / Jane Augustine.
p. cm.
ISBN 0-9713332-0-3
I. Title.
PS3551.U388 A89 2002
811'.54—dc21

2001006090

Marsh Hawk Press
PO Box 220, Stuyvesant Station,
New York, NY 10009
www.marshhawkpress.org

For Meg, Tom, Jeff, Pat,
Anthony, Felix, Philip, Daniel, Diego, and Leah

and

M.D.H., as always

# Contents

Part IV: **French Windows**

Part V: **On New York Time**

Heaven and earth are trapped in visible form:
all things emerge from the writing brush.

—*Wen Fu: The Art of Writing, III*
Lu Chi, 261-303 A.D.
(tr. Sam Hamill)


And he shewed me a pure river of water of life,
clear as crystal, .... and on either side of the river, was
there the tree of life

—*Book of Revelation 22: 1-2*
King James version, 1611

# PART I

# ARBOR VITAE

## Arbor Vitae

*at the house of a friend, Helen Wildman,*
*on Lake Paradox in the Adirondacks*

(i)

White apple blooms
outside the window
Below, a dark brook winds

White moon rises
above the pines—
window glass clean with rain

(ii)

Silent house, gray morning:
slow gaze wakes
silence of thought.

Wine-brown trillium,
triple sepalled, sprung
from its three-leaf stalk

sends a long filament
curving into the depth
of a glass vase.

Order, beauty in repose,
invisible growth.
Downstairs, a woman's voice

engineers action:

to plumb, wire, fix, wake up,
make it happen

(iii)

Yesterday— deathday of a friend
two years ago.  I forgot, busy

shopping with Helen's daughter,
half-blind, whose brain tumors recur.

That death: a suicide by pills.
The daughter cooks, mends, quilts

with her one good eye.  Helen cut down
overgrown trees that blocked

the view.  The blind girl looks across
the grayblue length of Lake Paradox.

She's ready to swim five miles,
a friend in a boat beside her.

The suicide's ashes: where are they?
Her last note: what did it say?

(iv)

Seen from a side window

gray fog obscures
the greening oaks

beyond the gray house

of Helen's brother—

Close to the glass
a slash of dark cypress branch.

(v)

In the farthest camp
under the pines
Helen's grandfather died.

East of its quiet,
a smaller camp looks over
a stilled silver cove.

Between them a meadow
of wild strawberry flowers.
Fruit to come, persisting ripeness

(vi)

*Arborvitae*, thick cedar,
stands on the brook's bank,

branching leaf from twig
too multiple to sketch

one by one, too elusive
en masse—
                    Last night

on the lake a low mist.

Watercolor
couldn't render

such metamorphosis
of water.
                    Still, the brush dips

once more, for Lu Chi wrote
          *When cutting an axe handle*

          *with an axe, surely the model*
          *is at hand.*

# PART II

# METAPHYSICS OF THE INTERIOR

# Snow on Horn Peak
*in the Sangré de Cristo mountains, Colorado*

Morning half cloudy, half clear.
Best pen lost.
      My oldest son, out of detox,

paints the pines in watercolor
from a palette long unused.
      Snow-melt feeds

blue fields of wild iris lower down.
Up here,  one gold mustard-bloom
      in leafy green

A small brush puts yellow

      in almost
      the right

      place.

## Swallows

Swallows swandive
under the eaves: cry *your house*
*is our house of air*


.     .


Where do I live?
        in Minnesota tomorrow
in the operating room
        with the infant grandson

    who almost died at birth


.     .


A wren whistles while
        I write near her nest.  Swallows'
white wingstroke gone

                into sky.

    .     .


Hearts of birds beat,
keep beating even without
        monitors' zigzag

    or watching eye.

# Metaphysics

if any, repose in grass this June;
dried wheat tufts suggest autumn.

Illusion of time: the view towards town
twenty years ago the same, one thinks,

the viewer changed but held, close
to hope, still doubting that green is only

made in the retina.
My son paints Winsor's Green
(Light) on Strathmore paper because *it is*

*that way*, and the world less doubtful
than one's thought of it — without

which it isn't ...
says who? Consciousness
is cellular, says Teilhard, in case

one should forget to bid the swatted cockroach
to become buddha.
Aggression won't

supply green. And could photosynthesis
produce ink for the poet's randomness which

hardly frames art, that neurosis skewing
acceptance?
Getting old? Well, resist

that thought as a reflex fed by newsprint.
But the physical transfixes an internal

metaphysical fear:  sooner to die
rather than later, as this cinquefoil's bright

yellow fades, and the chickadee
who sits on my boot-tip is surely not last year's.

Some fat chipmunk, however, steals
birdseed from the finches, and no intervening

helps.  Five droplets out of an overhead
cloudpuff threaten this page unpreventably

as the helpless face of any woman
crossing 23rd street at Second Avenue

to think a boon might come from bodies
of students shot in Tiananmen Square.
                                             Logic

won't de-corrupt governments, except
where a word properly lodges its depth

in the fluidity of things, which have a way
of constancy in greens of varying

grays — Payne's Light, for instance, for rocks
that stay mostly unseen, and yet crop out

holding landscape, or land-thought
resembling it, enough to wake you, caught out

in metaphysical blur — self-doubt, as if
good were invisible.  Wake you to get up and walk.

## Metaphysics II

Does a word hold a thing,
      a bowl of water reflecting
            the moon?  Thought, like water, exists

but slips out of form continually.
      This self too slips and falls
            within its shadow body till the final

disassembling.  Momentary brain-cells
      hold sun, moon, a few chemicals —
            what besides these holds all up-welling

history, memory?  The brain-bowl
      can contain more and more
            without enlarging.  When it goes

words stay, as on this page, and others.
      One spider's body exudes its web
            whose fine chain hangs and breaks, yet

these transient nets remain, the wish
      that the son who tans himself in this
            mountain air can hold his strength, can

live sustained, and that the grandson softly
      comes out of anesthesia to his father's
            relieving tears, the primal water

that ancient consciousness construed
      as "the deep" outside this universe
            — the deep within, bulking, confused,

seeing every possibility and object —
   mirrors, vices, seventy
      kinds of oak tree or creeping vetch —

in a single cell.
     So multiply made,
    I still think I'm alone, waiting
      for a phone call as if no one ever waited

before.  No end to desire's stirrings.
    This desire greens the tips of firs
      and makes the pump-motor click in

that one may turn a faucet and drink.
    At the end of phone lines intricately
      linked wait well-drillers, botanists,

one who writes, since one word
    prolongs the still-ephemeral.
      The observed absolute death of a cell—

do you credit those scientists?
    Yes.  And their connecting stays on
      after the end exists.

## Metaphysics III: After Waiting

"So the baby is fine," says my youngest son,
        phoning after the surgery, untroubled
as the day moon afloat in sunset clouds tinged

fiery on the under edge.  Rain gray dissolves
        above white billows, puffs.  Dusk's
long shadow-streaks make the valley more lovely.

                .        .

To wait— why give time
such power?  The not-yet
over now.  Privacy

of dream, the stream's depth
where fish swim
under ice which hides and protects.

To imagine grim
disorder, death out of place —
that's knowledge addicted

to form, to making
myself continue, to belief in omens,
false significance

as if a morning's rain
"meant" sadness to come, or a man's
dirty shirt "means" he's unclean—

the poet's error.  A blank
white envelope is simply unaddressed,
and light from a dead planet

not inferior or impure.
I take a fishhook off the line
and store it where it won't snag, or

not so badly, since I'm
still caught, and take the great
blue mountain-morning sky

personally, a good
infinite, intense, not my eye's
opening at all, not neutral

no more than the baby's
unexpected red hair and loyal
energy of his body's healing.

## At the Aspen Stump Again
*on hiking back up to Goodwin beaver ponds*

More worn, settled
      into the brown-bottomed pond
            which mirrors its clenched roots,

the stump accommodates wet
      grass-tufts, algae, the hot
            clarifying sun.  It leans to the blue

sky-reflecting water, less raw
      than years ago.  It's the season
            of early yellow-golden weeds like

dandelion, "false" lupine.  Currents
      hidden and swift ripple into green
            curves against the far bank.  Flies

skim the ex-addict's sunburned shoulder
      as he drops a fishline off a log.
            Trout hover near a sandshelf

undisturbed.  Repose.  Nothing to do — "no
      attainment and no non-attainment.."
            No pressure to move the mind

which doesn't slow any more than
      the exuberant diamond chilling
            stream rests.  It sends

its overflow into calm shallows.
      Sky sleeps there.  Tallest
            firs point downward — further,

stiller — and slow pine-smell
      sinks through the air.  The stump
      slopes jaggedly across the silted swamp

immoveable
        as some lost thought.

# Sunday Morning

(i)

No complacencies:
wren's nestlings hatched, flycatcher
poised on a dry pine tip—

Nature's not enough, no
mother, and illusory.
Sunfire produces

green contradictions: sky-
blue the shade of emptiness,
but benefits

blind motorbikers
as well as meditators,
death also growing

into the good, even if
TV commentators didn't
jiggle enameled eyes,

syllables, canned-pea
label in place of peas, hot
on a plate.
                    Desire
to be entertained —
what a mistake.  But desire

that cuts out its own
heart and tosses the pieces,
sunflower seeds to

the Steller's jays, that's
the sun that gilds emerald
the wings of bank-swallows

and polishes gravestones.

(ii)

All powers are higher, being real:

Every night of full moon
        led a lonely poet-monk northward,
          pinning haiku on cherry branches.

Tu Fu meditated in autumn
        while mountain winds wailed
          in the *wu-t'ung* trees

and Li Po leapt into a pool of wine.

I sit with pen and ink
        on the splintered wooden deck
        with this silent son, it seems

        recovering

Who can rely on the forms on pages
        that collapse into formlessness
        as bird-twitter in scrub oak

mixes into sough of wind and creek-water
        tumbling among white-blooming cresses

on the pump trail long untraveled?

Let's walk to the willow
       in which we saw a yellow-bellied sapsucker
       pluck beetles from a branch cleft

not "sucking sap" at all —

Think of form as emptiness:
       the cloudless sun at 10 a.m.


(iii)


*Accept the challenge which things present to words*
      —*Francis Ponge*


Blueflax miscalled "chicory,"
or periwinkle, blooms by the cabin steps:
blue or purple as that myrtle — or flowering
      myrrh? — in leafy banks

      under live oaks
and madrones at the old stone house in California,
where my father's study windows looked out
      over them.

      That room he sat in,
struggling to write. That dead father, his face
and voice held beyond photograph or scratchy tape
      on which he sang

*I did it my way*—

exact shading of the thing remembered,
     for which no word:

    Ephemeral petals fall by noon
beneath the stem whose furled buds englobe
    the blue to come.

\*\*\*

# Wind

sweeps through pine boughs.
Sough of water
over rocks: sound not

of wind but of wood,
stone resistance to
the unseen:

Word stirs dust off the leaf.
high clear dome
washed clean

*not I, not I but the wind —*

## Necessary

My son must leave today.
Flight scheduled on time.

Subdued light: a haze
dulls green mountainsides.

Blueflax petals, shades
bluer than sky, fallen in dry

grass. West wind may
soon brighten the snowpeaks

or it may not.
Lone flight of nighthawk.

Lone necessity to hang back
in rocky terrain.

## Exhausted

standing in the whirl
of inexhaustible wind,

twitter of birds,
cloud-shift:

dumbed eyes, ears register
endlessly. If

instead of clear, a mist
also wakes drifting

mind to heart's gist,
tenderness, a knowing, is

there a problem?
                    Miffed
because the roof-fixer's

late — so what? It's
a finite world. Dirt

scuffs up between rifts
in floorboards, sifts

from ceilings. Pay attention to inter-
stices. Do wash and pin it

on frayed line winter-
worn. Give in.

## Metaphysics of the Interior

Chilled gray sky lowers
        over the valley, and the mind
feels shutdown, mildly suffers.

Weather's not to be correlated
        with the personal: this diamond
intellect — anyone's — wakens

flash! like that, whatever
        light plays on it. Why
then this imagining of lessened

hearing, seeing? An inner scene
        crowds characters onstage,
who nag, rebut and disappear

a moment. Must write a letter,
        telephone, placate
them, hunch over the desk

indoors, keep after evasive
        freedom not obtained
by just this pursuit.
                The view

from the front window
        is blocked by the same
near-black pine, green a day or two ago.

# Clear Sky

High cool blue wind shakes
screen doors, wild roses, stones: clears
three words on a page.

Blanketflower, 'sugar-bowls'
bloom.  Can a rug be called meadow,
cup an acorn, the whole

world a house swept out,
dishes on the sink-board given
to whoever's around?

No greed to hold, or
less greed, wanting after all
a longer day, more

hours before the stars rise
through clean blackness, unpossessed.

## Moon and the Milky Way

(i)

Moon rising: a Chinese
bronze gong veiled in smoke

Cloud sinks: it brightens,
night's tiger's-eye

(ii)

After day's harsh wind
no sediment or blur between
mountains and sky

The river of stars flows over
pines in shadow whose tips
turn watery-black silver:

strongest light of far dark mind

## Broken Meditation

Late afternoon stillness:
        shadow of fir-tree and cabin's roof peak
fall over meadow and scrub oak.

A corner of sun on the deck,
        on a deer skull and tin pot, relic
of abandoned mine or Cottonwood hermit's

lost camp, signs to preserve
        of this mountain's history.  Serene
and glossy oak leaves glint, protecting

young firs among them.  This quiet
        opposes my jitters over property
in California, my dead mother's legacy.

Money troubles me, unsettles
        my thinking, as if, like the Chinese
poets, I too might be suddenly

exiled, deprived.
                The red
        bandana at my throat draws a sizzling
hummingbird to aim his beak

and I'm afraid he'll get me,
        cheat me like some west coast realtor
of something kin to that bureaucrat's security

which gave Tu Fu his brush. Yet
        he lost it, and seven mountains sealed
him away from the capital.

                              This free
I am also, with broken
           meditation and a few mosquitos
in a paintless chair whose rush-woven seat

was torn out twenty
           years ago by someone's kids.  Cheap
yellow rope replaces it and interweaves

with plastic straps.  Adequate
           as the sun goes and the last clouds clear
from sky even more absently blue-green

than an old scribe's agate
           inkstone whose repose freed him
for poetry and pointless dreaming.

# PART III

# THE CHANGES

## [Untitled: My Brother]

Again a cloudless morning:
      glazed-vase blue overhead
      a little too smooth,

dry stalks among green in the
      meadow, blanching dust on the old
      blocked driveway.  Into

this drought, concealed, arrives
      remnant of an angry dream
      as I stand on the deck

looking east into the glare too bright
      and the dust-haze on dim peaks:
      uprush of ancient resentment,

a half-broken open feeling, but
      of what?
            Disturbing, this lack
      of rain, this newscaster's "perfect

weather," as in the Napa valley
      in the seventies when my mother
      still lived there, distressed

by her lawn's dry patches marring
      the verdure, mottled like old skin—

Now my brother is driving in

      to stay for a week.  He's late,
      upset—

his rental car's     mudstreaked,
              has
       out-of-state     plates
because in Trinidad, or—
                   or California or some
                        place


someone made a mistake
        disturbing the carefully made plans
        which are his life's need.

But he's here, not fallen through
        the gap of fear, his shadow cast
        sharp against hillside weeds.

This mountain is a graveyard,
        its stones the bones of the dead.
        Our parents' dust flies

into the air under the hard
        parching sun. We two are left,
        disconnected. A gnarled pine

shades our greeting. A breeze,
        cool illusion, passes
        and I'm carrying my brother's bags,

helping him through the door. I see
        dust unswept at the doorsill.
        No excuse surely for wordless pain

when the day has this clarity
        and blue-green flowered curtains
        hang at the huge clean window.

## Stars: For My Father's Memory

Vega, Deneb, Altair—
starry arch to brace the night wall.

Past midsummer's height
dark lasts a little longer.

The fixed stars never fall.
Faintly they shine on the gravestones

at Rosita cemetery among
overgrown thorns.  My father died

on June 26, commanded
his ashes to be cast over the ocean.

No stone for him, for stars
to hover over, remembering.

Cold air, cold creek tumbling
beyond the dark trees,

a creek of stars overhead
to liven darkness.

## Cactus Flowering

Purplepink petals
on knobbled thorny antlers
of desert cacti

seen swiftly through
the windows of the airconditioned car:

petalled silks of the rich playgirl
next to the dustswept starving
Sudanese woman

on the TV screen.
One should stop, step out into

100-degree heat and get scratched
by those thorns.
I say to my brother,

"Look at the cactus blossoms
there — and there —"

He pushes his chin out
to look hard
but he can't see them.

## At Rosita Cemetery

Pine needles settle over
the old stones, the nameless ones:

incomplete families
behind a picket fence, birthdate

incised in marble.  No death
yet for a wife not visiting

a husband's grave on Sunday.
Here no chiselled deathdate

for Floye Smith, who, speechless,
strapped down, died March 6, 1987,

in a nursing home, her ashes not
here beside her suicide son's

despite her carved name waiting —

     So much for plans.

               So do I want
a northerly corner here
between a cracked red sandstone

marker, weather-shattered,
and the Adams child?

It's not important, just somewhere
someone might visit.
               I place two

fallen pine branches and five pine cones
at Floye's blank headstone,

having forgotten to bring flowers.

# Useless Stars

*after the evening news*

The stars oppose history,
shine on all atrocities

— the machine-gunned dead,
a ten year old abused

by her father, to whom a judge
gives her for custody—

Pity the poor
and the pain of the world

that the night, sweetsmelling
of eglantine, will not quell.

The stars offer no meaning.
Constellations have tricked

weak hopeful eyes. No hope:
the diamond light

cancelled out by daytime's
flat overwhelming white.

## "Genuine Heart of Sadness"

Birds twitter, sun
        again hot and clear outside. '
Mauve penstemon droops

in the vase.  Husband naps.
        I sit crosslegged on the dusty
rug.  My brother — how

to help?  Impossible —
        The room is curtained,
semi-shadowed,

quiet and unquiet.
        Heartless now to raise
a lofty hymn to diamantine day:

The flaw in the jewel —
        let it cleave open there.

## After Reading Tu Fu

Parched ground under day's-end sun,
long pine shadows over dry grass:
I pipe water to fir-tree roots,
write poems to bring blossoming
to purple lupine and scarlet gilia.
Mountain wind drifts to cities
where books rot in flooded basements.
It brushes this crescent moon rising westward.

"In the deepest water the fish's utmost joy."
In highest mountains empty purest blue.
A well a hundred feet beneath hard earth
draws from the source. A car passes,
kicks up neurotic dust. My son, why this
discontent, blaming others? Writing you,
I put aside the pen to watch the moon
sink behind Spring Mountain where the creek
                    comes down.

# Haiku at Midnight: At the Desk

Silence.  Curtains hang
      between the lightless room and
Saturn's splendid rings.

.  .

No sound.  Icebox hums.
      Husband sighs, reading in bed.
Pen scratches page, pauses

.  .

Speechless, my eyeglasses
      lie next to a small basket
woven of plain grass

.  .

Much paper, milfoil-
      white, to be thrown away, much
to bloom in meadows

.  .

To pacify the
      raucous red paste-jar, one must
turn off the late lamp

.  .

Desire!  You keep pens
      in jars, and the gauzy veil flung
across the unseen overhead.

# Once More At Rosita Cemetery

(i)

An old man stakes out the plot
for my grave. His frail arm lifts
a sledge hammer too heavy for it,

almost driving a pipe into the ground
with my name on it, not yet
memorial. In his soft gentleman's

voice he speaks of history,
his Civil War forebears, some for
the North, some for the South: "You know,

even afterwards the Southerners
were still convinced they were right —
couldn't persuade them to think otherwise."

Opinion hard as Barre granite.
History alleviates, can't cancel. "We
buried a baby here. And over by those trees

our plot —" And then he's pleased
to see the sunburnt blond-bearded
worker come to help him clear

fallen pinecones and prune back
wayward mountain mahogany. It's late
in the morning. They'll work all day

tidying graves, for those on both sides.

(ii)

Dawn thought:
      meet the gentle old man
            under the benign
Rosita pines

Noon thought:
      grandson coming to stay in the cabin —
            the sun
past meridian

Night thought:
      Why afraid? Consciousness
            doesn't make much
of itself, touches
      lightly, breaks off,
            resumes.

Evergreens spread
      dry needles, a sign
            that they live
for a while.

# Rain

freshens grass-tips, not
deeper.  Still a fire danger
in higher forests.

Dry holds underground
at the parched roots, more than
depression dust, fear.

Can poems help the mind
lying in wilderness, an
unbanked campfire?

Lightning opens low
steel-gray clouds.  Thunder
rattles the doorframe.

More rain will soak in
to the meadow still half straw
and stunted blanketflower,

cut a runnel straight
downhill.  Dry hearts, they're
passing you — the hungry

black man at McDonald's door,
the rag-heap sleeping on
the railroad station floor.

## Heat Lightning

*for the infant sleeping*

Lightning plays in night clouds
to the east. Moon and stars in clear
dark overhead. No choice

.      .

Still pine shadows crisscross
silver meadow, silver road. Child
sleeps under silver roof

.      .

Wild silent light dances
protection over farm-lights, its
timid imitators.

.      .

Night-obscured mountains,
books, ink on paper, patience —
these let me sleep

like the little boy growing
between thunderheads over
far mining towns

and the talus slope
always to be climbed.

# By Moonlight

Moon on high: a stone
in the lake of the sky
invites a diver

as into an ocean
to go deep, deeper
to grasp a lighted world,

dive to rise
up through trees
of black coral,

a sea-creature
foreign to daylight,
its dry perverse pain,

drawn to the crystal eye
which changes,
truthful as dream.

# Darkness

No stars but blackness past
      the porchlight's pale angle along
the wet grass.  No sign:

eyes strained from typing,
      wrist arthritic.  Night trees drip
invisible.  That black cloud

blocks off what stage?  It's
      after midnight and I'm not
finished.  What made me think at dawn

of twenty years ago, my homemade
      olive green skirt and roundcollared
print blouse, when the kids

slept in double cot-bunk beds
      behind olive green curtains
next to shelves of treasures,

crayons, mica-stones —
            that *déjà vu?*

# Late

Scorpio low in the south,
      Antares caught in a pine branch,
        Vega's moved

only slightly past zenith.
      Mind of quiet night expands
        midsummer's gem

at heart. A painter friend,
      her hair gone white,
        opaque stone—lapis—

in her wedding band,
      had her wallet stolen: "nothing
        but driver's license

and 53 cents." Knows "changes
      must come —maybe drawing
        is what I do best."

Care for an old man
      in an old house brings
        her foot to the same threshold

daily. Fixed starlight's slight sheen
      on an unnoticed
        windowsill.

*****

# PART IV

# FRENCH WINDOWS

# From a Paris Sketchbook

Eiffel Tower over
plane trees, sidewalk tables,

smooth green lawn between paths
where nannies watch infants

roll balls, jump rope:   *La Grande
Jatte moderne*, serene.


     .     .     .

Place de la République
     at midnight. Amber *phares*
circle past cafés, pink
     fringed shades, geraniums
in boxes. A couple
     lean together, head to head.


     .     .

On the boulevard a *flâneur*
     in shirtsleeves strolls
among tree-shadows, flicks
     a cigarette away, passes
into a dark sidestreet. Music from
     an unseen jukebox.


     .     .

Darkness overhead. Who can see
     moon or stars when floodlights
burnish golden flanks
     of warriors' horses rearing
before the door of the *Cirque d'Hiver*
     posed in continual sun?

## Notre Dame de Blanc-Manteaux
### *in the Marais*

Our Lady in dulled aura
of uncleaned gold opens

accepting hands over the
holy book and microphone.

Clear plastic covers the
holy table's old lace —

no great light here
from the pallid clerestory.

Confession hour: the booths
empty, ecclesiastical chat

from some back room.  Large
Renaissance Virgin's jarred

from her frame.  By Vincent
de Paul's bust a display

of children's crayoned offerings:
*Jésus ressuscité: Je crois, crois-tu?*

Yes, I do—in the chipped paint
and one or two candles

in the brune disintegration,
slow sinking of too hard a floor.

# Interior: Midnight
### 8, rue du Grand Prieuré

In the nursery, the hand-sewn quilt
that wrapped my daughter's infant son
and red knit pants outgrown sit stacked

on shelves. He's walking now,
wears bigger shoes. Tomorrow in the south
I'll see him, changed from the round

soft outdated photo-baby.
Stocking dolls my grandmother made
for me—and I played with them—

stand on a corner shelf. She
and her daughter have vanished.
My hair is graying. Where's my handwork?

At Musée Carnavalet, unknown painters
recorded the blood poured away
under stones I stepped across today

in the Place de la Bastille,
thinking them neutral, ordinary
like me, blank.
                    To record:

this stitch outlasts the hand that sewed.
His eye will read, or hers—whose?
Whoever wants to know the revolution

continuing, doing and undone.

## In the Dark Garden — 10:30 p.m.
### *Rabastens, near Toulouse*

We sit under acacias' feather leaves
after a passing storm.  Crickets creak
in far fields a language both French
and English.  Open shutters bring
cool into small bedrooms beneath
whose windowsills sleep hydrangeas
and begonias.  One cry from the
child's crib; he turns over, sleeps again.

Another child next spring.
Overhead the quiet stars.

## Siesta: Entr'acte

Big fly buzzes from
       back garden to front terrace
over this table.

I mended a hole
       in an unneeded sweater.
Sunflowers turn straw

on the hill. This sun's
       a heavyweight winner; I
demand another bout.

Rebellious mind wants
       up. Old body sweats. On the
terrace, purple, mauve,

pink-rose petunias,
       begonias wine-red-leaved
in russet pots, more

hot-headed than the sun.

       I sketch
          *rose de rosier de*
          *Rabastens, oeillet rouge — ni*
            *mots ni l'encre inclus*

## At a Rainy Window, 2 p.m.

Gray-black clouds move north, shift south
over the cathedral and the cemetery.

The baby can't stop his temper tantrum.
Parents' feet pass up and down the hall.

French flag flies above the Occitanian
crusaders' cross, gold on red,

a heart-struggle still after eight centuries.
*Une guerre d'annexion*, king and pope

joined their powers against independence
of spirit. *Esprit* equals "mind" in French.

But in Tibetan, mind lives in the heart center.
It thinks before words.  A nephew plays

with his uncle in the garden where trees
still drip heavy with rain.  Sun arrives,

temporary, maybe.  It's dawn in Minnesota
where a daughter-in-law starts chemotherapy.

Which power wins, hope or history?

Roses bloom for no reason.  Appreciate!
Appreciate!  Here comes another buzz of rain

which means take an umbrella while traveling.
And it's nearly time to go — the child

to his nap, cancer-ridden girl to her doctor,
and I to what, under what flag of lost causes

in a country thick with mosses, aged trees,
fields of weed where swallows nest in stones

from *châteaux* fallen in the fifteenth century.

## Late Summer Meditation

Voices from the garden after rain:
two little girls exclaim over the hydrangeas.
My daughter sews during the infant's siesta.
I sit in the breezeless bedroom,
fertile damp soaking my fingers and eyebrows.
Grapes and tomatoes ripen in the farm-plot.
In this countryside, a horn of plenty:
Other lives complete. Loneliness of thought solo —
                the best *donnée*.

# After Ponge

(i)

The abyss between word and thing is total. Human
desire makes it bridgeable. But it must be the right
bridge, delicate and strong, a *pont neuf*. Is it always
poetry? Is it worth disputing the label? The deepest
desire is to speak the unspeakable. But these depths
don't contain sin or evil. The unsaid is not the unsayable.
The unconscious can open with simplicity; it's honorable,
itself and not something imposed or external. The *real*
word both touches upon and creates reality. Nor should
it necessarily be called art.

Ponge's carnation: *oeillet*. Oyez oyez: hear, hear. For a
child one points to an object. The carnation, *oeillet*, is a
bridge between word and thing. But "carnation" and
"oeillet" have nothing to do with each other, or the
flower garden.

(ii)

The abyss between word and thing isn't total, or there
would be no need to search for *le mot juste*, would there?
Is this right word closer to 'the thing?' But what 'thing'?
A word is also a thing.

(iii)

A word
is also a sound,
a violin
from the next room.

If  Beethoven, deaf,
heard his music,
isn't a poem
evolved in the silence
      between
        the farthest stars?

## In Provence, Near Venasque: Le Beaucet

After a dusk climb
to the ramparts
of a ruined castle,

sad Catalan music
on a guitar
half-badly played

before the altar
of the little church
under repair—

       old paintings stacked
       under a dusty sheet
       lean crookedly,

       bug-killer sprayed
       for concertgoers' benefit
       stings the eyes,

       a missed note or four
       on a dead string—

       At intermission
       on the unlit parapet
       the guitarist smokes, shaky.

The battlement's rubble settles deeper..
Young volunteers, they say,
are fixing the church.

     Art is a skewed composure

of what isn't yet mastered,
    a dismembered past,
        disarrangement.

Tarnished gilt on a nameless statue— let it stay.

# A Failed Watercolor of the House at Venasque

False eye evens out
    the house too rectilinear
        to start with.  Crude color

and square brush in a child's
    paintbox dab at contrast,
        wall-shadow, but the vast

light won't be confined.
    Would-be painter is the slave
        of external sensation

mistaken for the "real."
    But all materials are good,
        workable, even this room,

tight and heating up
    as the Midi afternoon
        comes on —

    *straight black line out of the picture*
    *on the right: electric wire, or the phone*
        *— a mistake — no tie-line*
    *from daughter to mother*

I didn't clamp it
    to the pale stone façade, but
        it has to be there,

not the worst part of the composition.

## Stone Water-Trough at a Crossroads in Provence

Between Venasque and Saint-Didier
    fresh water drips continually
        into a basin that overflows
            into a *lavoir* beyond the pillar.

Off of rough slopes, breezes
    from vineyards with ripening grapes
        ruffle the plane trees' fat leaves.
            Cool of oncoming autumn.

Rocks are loosening in the slopes
    ready to fall into crumbling gullies
        among banks of drying golden stubble,
            weeds and live oak.

It is 1950 in the Napa valley
    at Stonehouse where my mother gardens
        in overalls, her long hair
            tied with a shoestring, and my

father sits at the picnic table
    reading *The San Francisco Chronicle*—
        Bells of Saint-Didier sound from
            Mont La Salle, the monastery's

blue-tiled tower above the trellised grapevines
    of the Christian Brothers,
        from whom we get—my father smiles—
            our water and our wine.

## In Paris Again

Cool autumnal blue
sky over narrow streets, more
cool in long shadow

    .    .

*at the Musée d'Orsay*

Sober Cézanne: brown
table, gray pitcher, fruit, white
napkin struck by strange light

His apples pour across
a blue-flowered cloth.  In my daughter's kitchen
tomatoes in a cobalt bowl

on faded mauve African batik
beside uncurtained windows

    .    .

*at Café Procope*

On the sidewalk by the
back door where revolutionaries
stepped, a red-faced
body sleeps stretched out
in grease-black suit, shoeless
smiling a little
as in America, inventor of revolutions

    .    .

Reading Segalen's *Voyage to the Country of the Real*,
imagined as he traveled in China in 1914,
so I go down steep stairs into the metro
                at St-Michel

.          .

Standing behind the great *horloge*
    of the museum, time appears
        reversed over the Seine which flows
           brightly in its unchanged
                direction.

.          .

*the next day*

Gray light behind
livingroom drapes, but open windows
show clear sky again.

Clarity comes back
if time does not: a tangled dream
no more real, nor less,

than light whose space seems
eternal. Time to take off
a faded nightdress, put on

a shirt bright as bougainvillea
and white summer sandals
to walk the city

whose sewers one may
visit, study how the water
of the Seine collects

its filth, is filtered
and re-cleaned,
continues its collecting.

# In A Dream My Mother

appears in a chartreuse suit,
      tells me she couldn't find
the right shoes:

I shout, "She's alive — proof
      of physical resurrection!"
I walk with her, convinced truly.

Then by Canal Saint-Martin
      she sits down on a bench,
slumps, eyes closing.  She's going back

to death's place, inaccessible.

Waking, not loss
      but opening of unseen connection
is the dream's sense—

      Haunted all day— *Chartreuse de Parme,*
           the drink,  a charterhouse,
           her Girl Scout oxfords,
           my foot pain —

Sitting late in a street café
      I try to tell my husband
how good it was, the dream,

and start to weep.

# After the Museums, By a Window,
## Late Afternoon

*Prajña*, knowledge,
    mothers the mind.
        Empty sky provides

birthing space.  Wind
    rises, collects
        bits of grit,

a crumpled paper
    or two, passes
        them on.  In

the museum relics
    of a bishop's cope,
        signature

of a tormented poet.
    Everyone dies.  Daughter
        will listen to

dream-mother's words
    alive, remember as she
        hears the streetsweepers

brushing up debris
    first thing
        in the morning.

## *Une Américaine à Paris*

World of another language —
　　　is it so unlike the American,
　　　　　so word-made?

Narrower sidewalks, cleaning men
　　　in green uniforms with green brooms,
　　　　　odd electric switches,

water-heaters— these no longer multiply
　　　differences.  Street-noise the same.
　　　　　A mother in the park

bawls out the bigger boys who push
　　　the littler.  Sunlight.  The faces stare.
　　　　　Paris doesn't make

all Parisians happy, either.
　　　The well-coifed sun-bronzed woman
　　　　　in sunflower gold linen,

patent pumps to match, looks off into air
　　　as she passes.  At home, backs to each other,
　　　　　my daughter and I sit reading.

*Larousse* by me slowly aids
　　　decoding of *Libération* but doesn't help
　　　　　break down the wall between

thought and speech.  But thought too
　　　fails.  Voices in the street — I can't hear
　　　　　nor catch the tone —

fear, pleasure? — to which I want
  to respond. *Plein air* alone,
      what words make the transformation?

# The Louvre:  Egyptian Antiquities

Early morning.  No one around the ground-floor tomb,
the *mastaba* of a man of means, a stonewalled room.
Thus I'm alone as he was at the house of death when troops
of women singlefile with slim white-draped hips brought fruits
of every kind—dates, figs—vegetables, grains to sooth
his life-hunger, and men lined up to bring him each a goose,
a hare, a fish, for death could not be very different.
                                    They made known
the way into the unknown eternal by carving it in lasting stone.

The seated scribe, androgyne, sees into some far space.
He has high cheekbones, a straight spine. A scroll
lies across his lap. The words to come are essential. Wait.
Hieroglyphs dictated to the carver give testimonial
that the dead aren't so, entirely.
                                    What then to leave in place
for those whose desert tombs are rubble, utterly effaced?

## À Bientôt

September.  Chill breeze.
      7 p.m.  Clouds rosy under
gray at the end of

rue St.Antoine.  We
      to New York tomorrow, our hosts
to Moscow Monday.

World scattering: last smile
      from the infant a voluble
break—
        Not to take

possession means to
      keep on longing.  How can sky,
that nothingness through

which we'll fly, connect?
      *Emptiness also is form.*
A daughter isn't

her mother; all genes
      are accidents passed on.
Stone arches of the

ancient Place des Vosges,
      then high modern cream façades,
shelter what kind of

 midnight?

# PART V

# ON NEW YORK TIME

# Re-Entry

*New York, 8:50 p.m. 3 September*

(i)

POW!　out of JFK Air France terminal a/c, oy vey
　　　94 degree heat, dirt, crowd on steamy sidewalk
under
　　　　　the Carey Bus sign.　Zigzag taxis, vans,
　　　　　　　bunged-up autos illegally zoom
into the bus lane, blue-shirted cop yowls
　through bull-horn.
　　　　　Ongoing oncoming zany headlights flash
on heaped luggage carts.　　Late　bus comes;
passengers crush in till jampacked.
　　　Angry-faced redhead dame curses young black
woman bus driver:
　　　　"You
　　　　　pushed me off　this bus! I'll
report you! I must get on this bus!　My luggage is on this
bus!　I hurt my back pushing my luggage
　　　into the baggage compartment ..."

　　She's off.　We're off.
　　　　Gross dark bleeds over the agitated
highway.
　　　　A migraine.

　　　　No pill for it.

(ii)

East 18th street:

ripped-open black plastic garbage bag
        on the sidewalk covered by heaps
    of greasy bags, pizza box, plastic wrappers,
used diapers leaking infant turds onto a pizza
    half-eaten.  Bums got
        the 3 or 4 bottles returnable
        for 5 cents each.

Kid off the stoop toddles
    into the oilslick gutter-water.

(iii)

Oh Paris!  Azure sky over the still canal
        and calm barges as an elevated train
swings away from the Place de la Bastille—

On Boulevard Richard Lenoir the foul marketplace
        at sunset—staved-in boxes, stinking fruit and
fishscraps. Darkfaced Algerians slowly swept it up.

(iv)

*Le trottoir, c'est moi,* this sidewalk crowd.

        Hobbling old gal in fuschia polo shirt
        and slacks smiles too broadly
        under her gray friz and white sunhat.

Post-insomnia depression.  Too late!  Too

late!  Hurry to catch up with the overwrought
competitor—who?  In whose
oncoming eyes a threat?

My concrete heart and feet
      of tar, hard, hurt.  Wrenched
      a wrist muscle tugging my luggage—

            Mind kicks up
this garbage and the frowning face
of the plump blonde with germanic hair

braided across her head in peasant style,
      coming at me.  Her ancient hunchbacked mother
      clings to her in pain

            But no:  the braid is a
twisted scarf.  I didn't see it right,

    not all of it.

(v)

Well, did you think you could always vacate?
The pseudo-organized employee goes out
      to understand New York:

    2-story brick facades
above shop signs LOCKSMITH
      FISH MARKET—
          Deformed lettering
in cartops' bent mirrors
      recede down the avenue.

Accurate data mistaken,
        too much for the eye
        too large for an idea.

                        (vi)

It is late in the day.

Pressures.  Sweaty

breath crushes the chest.
100% humidity.

Slick skin drips.

Mad eyes
of the Citibank beggar,

crocodile eyes
of the well-dressed dean

on the campus path
between untrimmed thorn bushes

and a Civil War cannon
aimed at the bursar's office

welcome my return.

# East Hampton, Long Island: Nearly Midnight

Wind stirs leaves overhead
in darkness.  Insects unseen whir
steadily.  Peepers vibrate a half-tone.

Are there stars?  Myopic
eyes see the same blackness closed
or open, conditioned by light

on desks, checkbooks.
Eyes cast their purplish fever against
the eyelids, trying to substitute or

evade the quiet lack
of definitions.

         Night: I'll never
give up loving poetry,
its steady uselessness.

## The Next Midnight, Even Quieter

Afternoon in the mind's eye:

how silver-blue water
lapped the beach
under pale blue sky silvered

with cirrus, how white sails
reached slowly over
the silenced mirror

where gulls dozed as if
summer ease might stay.

     And now the tree-frogs
     also sleep
     and asters in the centerpiece
     suggest an autumn

dusk—and goldenrod
extra-tall at roadside
darkens its flashy pollens.

     A cycle of vanishing:   at the beach
     ebullient orange rosehips
     where the roses pinked the tangle

     and these darken too.

# A Cornucopia on Columbus Day

*in East Hampton, remembering my mother*

Born 92 years ago October 12,
died on my birthday three years ago.

Her crystal birds, fat as tears
sit on my shelves as they sat
on hers in the nursing home.

> In the jewelbox's drawers lie heaps
> of earrings she searched among to match
> her outfits, red, green, gold —

>> plastic fruits, hoops,
>> tiny globes of
>> no intrinsic value

but to make the road still curve
past hilly California vineyards
where the grapes grow purple—

> In this morning's chill
> I cut the wild grape's tendrils'
> fruitless grip

> on the young *arborvitae*,
> which must stand sturdy in winter,
> and heaped the yellowing vines

> around the front-porch pumpkins
> not yet cut with a child's ghost face
> for All Saints eve.

>> No need
>> to cut the bittersweet —
>> later it bears
>> red berries.

## Note in a Sketchbook

Grapevine and bittersweet
intertwine.  Bugs eat both.  Veins
show intricate

against light, yellow
at edges.  No end to tight
grasping tendrils, drying,

stray twigs caught.

## Eleventh Day, Eleventh Month

Went out in keen sun
this afternoon to cut
bittersweet's orange-red berries
from bare twigs where
cool wind shuffles leaves across a
lost lawn, an ocean tossing
brown waves, shape of Hokusai's
spume curl or Van Gogh's sky.

Autumnal art of fading:
one cell melts into another laid
under the moment's microscope.
One face among thousands opened
into a camera as the Berlin Wall
came down.
                So much falling
reaches the core.  So many leaves
I watch at 2 a.m., sleepless,
as they gleam in the moon's spotlight,
knifed by iron tree-shadows
faintly rustling under
the suddenly brilliant stars.

## Before Departure

To travel, to go beyond —
    only a quick flight
to snowy Minnesota

but to go, to leave,
      to separate:

      Only a few minutes before I stepped
      into the California hospital room,
            my mother's breath had stopped.
    her mouth the hard O
    I sat beside—
              Only
      a moment of going,
         invisible the breath,
      then no breath:

    Oldest son's sad voice
        phoning from Saint Paul:
    "Michelle's not getting better..."

I pack quickly, to fly

yet every day I leave
    some clothes behind,
notes on my desk

*bring, do, write ...*
    string of words on the page
for them to find.

## NYC Again: On Return

Gray light through
        the back window.  Dull roar of
                trucks on First Avenue.

A scrawled list
        on the desk under the light's
                eye-beam: do [this]

or [that].  Phone
        rings, irritated boss: "... conflicts
                in my department over

your concert..."  so
        I must dress, go, soothe—

                *Nodes of anger*
                        *block the connecting lines,*
                *subways, flight courses, pattern*
                        *of the Australian natives'*
                *songs by which their ancestors*
                        *in the Dream-time sang*
                *the world into being—*

Here's a "sort of song":
        impulse along a line across
                America, a neural web of mind,

these scenes conjured
        as if on a TV screen:
                one son sleeps on a sofa
                near his sick wife's bed, another son
                feeds his infant boy.

Around them sweep
      winds that carry all away—
            but not yet.
                    Phone lines sway

and the radio blips
      the dead of the morning,
            murders, weather, the traffic

jams, thousands of stopped
      cars. In each, the driver
            seethes: *I, I alone, must go on.*

## Insomnia:  the Darkness

cuts into day-life's logic,
      wakes up another mind,
           the one that won't belong

to schedules.  To live now
      in the unlit hallway, kitchen
           where the streetlight-haunted window

rattles, to think how
      living is remembering — memory
        wakes you:

                *Don't forget*
    *how yesterday the little grandson*
    *ran his red truck along the brick wall —*
    *or fifty years ago the father*
    *strung the Christmas lights*
    *and one, a blue parrot with a yellow beak,*
    *shone in the fir branches*

              not long ago but now

in the timeless dark
      that floats you like amnion.

      Dark egg of the world,
how you open, how within you
      genes infinitely continue
           to multiply —

## Fiery Sunset

in coldest December
over the wilderness beach —
sky-curve of fire and gray purple cloud edge.

Night broods, stretches
above it. Fire lies on the water,
shrinks and pales. The off-sea wind blows

freezing. Lurid sensation and pain
I'd say — too much. No regret
to their going,
        but I'd be lying..

Light vanishes. We stumble back
along a crooked path among tree trunks
heavily bent over, bodies of night.

A small moon muzzled by mist
hangs in a branch as black as this
lampless earth, and lights it

        *Loss of my body*
        *threatens me. If only*
        *I can hold such fire a while —*

Delusion. One goes, and others go.

But now remember how it happened,
that gift, much more
than ever could have been desired.

# Veil

Snow is falling again.
    The driveway light shows
a white membrane blurring

yew shrubs and leafless oaks,
    ghost flesh that vanishes.
I turn off the light, begin

to take on that ending.

    .    .

Deep snow by morning.
    A blizzard.  I rush crazy
into the cold white

beating against my face.
    Got to catch a train,
got to get there—leave my house

of shelter to struggle,
    fight.  A frantic windshield-wiper
doesn't clear my sight.

Wind piles drifts
    against the padlocked
railroad station door

and the train doesn't come.
    Mad Azerbaijani shot Armenians
to get their apartments

screaming Allah! Allah!
    Carry a gun, meet a gun.
This aggression carries into snowfall:

am I also insane, blind and buried
    by the inner avalanche?

## Late Afternoon, East Hampton

Leaving soon.  A pause,
    nervous, before getting on
        to the next thing

as if that not-yet-done
    weighs more than
        this flighty now?

    Walked to the beach
    to gaze across the moss-gray sound
    to the north shore's minute ridges

    Wanted to keep these
    in my eye, not leave,
    not leave finally

    the frame whose screen
    of skin falls cell by cell
    into the shower drain

    with loose hairs not
    to be replaced on the
    stubborn skull believing

    in long life.

So a timer will click
    the night light on for safety.
        A machine will speak my voice
as if I'm here.  Can't postpone going
    to the train, whose iron step
        will not give way

    as I lift my baggage in.

# Endgame

*(Purkhang: temporarily constructed ceremonial oven
for cremation of Tibetan lamas)*

Hiked that last retreat day
the rutted road under evergreens
whose black branches kept
massive snowmounds frozen,
slick, blocking the log-roads,
feet slipping till I slowed
and held each step with care
not to break a leg crossing
till ice became mud and the way
widened out of deep gloom
into a field where the *purkhang* stands,
isolated, white-plastered, square
on a lonely rise, bare bone against green,
its four oven mouths shut tight
facing the four directions,
its chimney-tower pointing
into directionless gray space
whose cold winds whirl
a torment of wet flakes
out of the bowed fir-tree tops
tangled and overgrown at the
shaggy meadow's edge that backs off
from the cremation place.

     Here the remains of a body
that had once held a mind
and had decomposed to water
packed in salt had gone to fire
and then to air (but not this air

of now) and in that air set
an arc of gold, two arcs, green-tinged,
the hoped-for rainbows in the smoke
created by the logs of *arborvitae*,
cedar, sacred fuel of enlightenment.

The fire has long been out.
White paint peels from the ledge
where a few dry flowers lie
and coins, a velvet hairpin
disintegrating in the weather.
They offered what little they had
thought up on the spur of the moment
at this temporary furnace, reminder
of a transient life declaring transience
the rule, as everyone knew and knows
and won't admit, so to gaze fixed
on this crumbling structure is deluded
and generally useless—

A sudden furious flurry of snow
whips its wild white scarves
around the white pinnacle:
      *such a thunderstorm will not*
      *come again soon.*

Of you, my world, I got an eyeful. Your turbulence
isn't internal. You cry aloud: get up,
go, why are you waiting around
      as if your heartbeat were not sufficient?

# Heat

abnormal for March
      brings yellow and purple crocus
            into the pigeon-lawn

at East 16th Street.
      From Paris my daughter telephones:
            the *petit-fils* born Sunday

sleeps at her side.
      Can one dismiss from mind
            so soon those blinding

winter snowstorms?  Uniformed
      workers prune the excess
            branch-tangle over the grass,

startling the pigeons off
      their brightly blossoming carpet.

# Night

*(insomnia: reprise)*

Night wind shakes the old window.
What thought lies beyond the wall?

I was scrubbing spots off the floor,
making a list of things to forget.

The frustration of mirrors: a door
is what's wanted, an opening.

The room widened and darkened
under the same mundane ceiling light.

Breath, ah—the wind lifts
the curtain, unseen, the transformer.

So late to be transformed and left
the same, shaky, rattling in the frame.

# At 5:45 p.m. before Good Friday on East 18<sup>th</sup> Street

To close the book:
      regret, accept the sun's decline
behind the hospital tower.

To open another book:
      meet morning sun with denial
of afternoon. The gold lilies flower

long in a pale green vase,
      longer than expected, a sturdy
buddha-bronze gold

that oxidizes slowly.
      Ink also lasts long on closed pages.
To read invites decay

as exposure to light ruins fine art.
      Still, one wants always to keep on
reading by a good night light

till the book must drop away —
      Infuriating even to think
of tiring. It is still day.

The sun still shines on Horn Peak.
      Wind riffles the watercolor paper.
Another painting to be made.

Underground, wild iris, *fleur de lys*,
      deepen their blue. Soon
it will cover the mountain.

**Jane Augustine** has published three chapbooks, *Lit By the Earth's Dark Blood*, *Journeys*, and *French Windows*, a much-anthologized short story "Secretive," and poems in many literary magazines. Winner of two fellowships in poetry from the New York State Council on the Arts, she also has a Ph.D. with specialization in modern women writers. She is the editor of *The Gift by H.D.: The Complete Text* (University Press of Florida, 1998) and has taught at Pratt Institute, The New School, and Naropa University. She lives in New York City and Westcliffe, Colorado.